Once you've seen one Santa, you've seen... The Mall.

Stocking Stuffers for Adults and Kids: Christmas Dad Jokes Illustrated

A Dad Joke Parody Joke Book

I0170062

ISBN: 978-1-7361214-2-9

First printing, 2023.

Roger Schroeder
Colorado Springs, Colorado, 80910

Support@sofakingrad.com

To:______________________________

From:____

____

____

What did one snowman say to the other one?

"Do you smell carrots?"

Knock, knock. Who's there?
Olive. Olive, who?

Olive (all of) the other reindeer.

What does Santa use to clean his sleigh?

Comet.

Where do snowmen keep their money?

In a snow bank.

Knock, knock. Who's there?
Murray. Murray who?

Murray Christmas!

If anyone out there will be eating Christmas dinner alone because they have no family or friends, please message me.

I need to borrow your chairs.

What do snowmen like to do on the weekend?

Chill out!

What's the difference between Santa's reindeer and a knight?

One slays the dragon, and the other's draggin' the sleigh.

What is green, white, and red all over? over?

A sunburnt elf!

Nobody likes Christmas carolling with Yoda.

One for The Pilots:

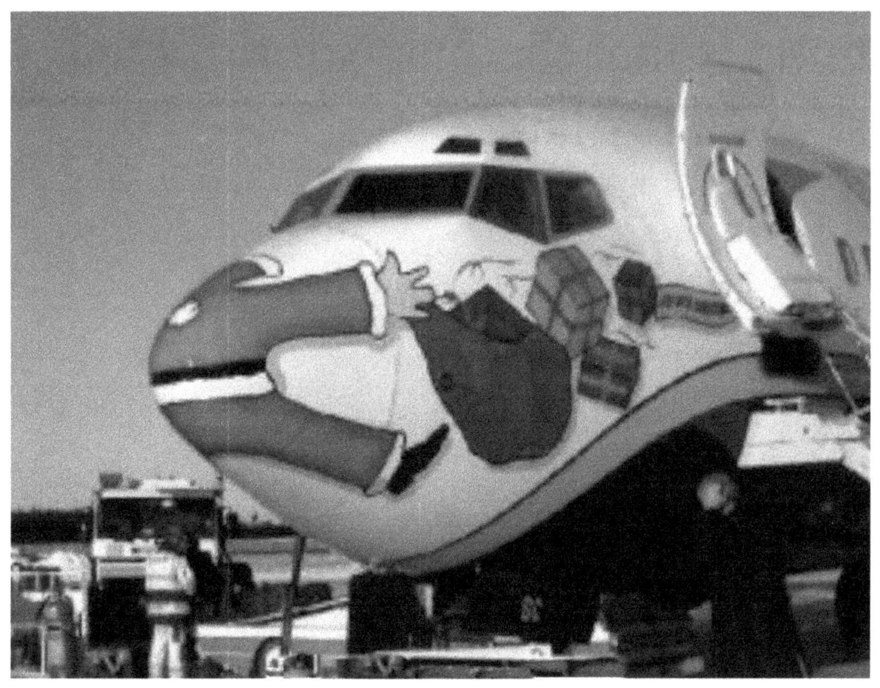

Santa Clause, his reindeer, and his sleigh are at the airport for his annual pilot re-certification. After passing his ground test, the FAA representative tells Santa to get into to the sleigh to go for a check ride with him.

Continued →

As Santa gets into the sleigh, he notices that the inspector has a rifle on his lap.

Continued →

Santa asks, "what's that for?"

The rep cocks his gun and says, "well Santa, typically, we are not allowed to tell you information prior to the flight check, but on this flight you're going to lose an engine."

What do you get if you cross an iPad with a Christmas tree?

A pineapple!

What has a jolly laugh, brings you presents, chases mice, and scratches up your furniture?

Santa Claws.

What do you get when you cross a snowman and a dog?

Frostbite.

Why was Santa's little helper depressed?

Because he had low elf esteem!

What do you call an old snowman?

Puddles

Why did Santa go to music school?

So he could improve his wrapping skills

What did the cow say on Christmas morning?

Mooooey Christmas!

What goes “oh, oh, oh”?

Santa falling backwards!

What do monkeys sing at Christmas?

Jungle bells, jungle bells!

Which of Santa's reindeer has bad manners?

Rude-olph!

대기

What do you sing at a snowman's birthday party?

Freeze a jolly good fellow!

What Christmas carol is heard in the dessert?

Oh Camel all ye faithful!

How did the police know that Rudolph was drinking while he was driving Santa's sleigh?

His red nose

Did you know that chickens are better at marketing than turkeys?

Have you ever heard of a Kentucky Fried Turkey?

Why are Christmas trees bad at knitting?

Because they always drop their needles.

What do you get when you cross a bell with a skunk?

Jingle smells!

What nationality is Santa Claus?

North Polish.

Why does Santa have three gardens?

So he can ho ho ho!

What do you call a snowman gardener?

Frosty the Mow-man!

Why did the elves ask the turkey to join the band?

Because he had the drum sticks!

What does the Christmas tree say to the light bulb when it's sad?

Lighten up!

What did the Gingerbread Man put on his bed?

A cookie sheet!

Why are there only snowmen and not snow women?

Because only men would stand out in the snow without a coat.

How much did Santa pay for his sleigh?

Nothing, it was on the house!

What do schools of fish sing during the winter?

Christmas Corals!

What did the reindeer say when he saw an elf?

Nothing, reindeer can’t talk.

When does Christmas come before Thanksgiving?

In the dictionary!

Which elf was the best singer?

ELFis Presley.

What's red, white and blue at Christmas time?

A sad candy cane!

What is a snowman's favorite lunch?

An Iceberger!

MISSING
ELF

I hate when the elves help decorate the tree.
NICKEL

What do you call a snowman with a six-pack?

The abdominal snowman.

How does Rudolph know when Christmas is coming?

He refers to his calen-deer.

What do you call a greedy elf?

Elfish.

What does an elf study in school?

The elfabet.

What How does a sheep say Merry Christmas in Spanish?

Fleece Navidad!

What does Santa do when the reindeer drive too fast?

Hold on for deer life.

Who delivers presents to dogs?

Santa Paws!

It possesses the same full-bodied flavor of the toilet bowl, yet has a distinctive woodsy taste...

How do sheep greet each other at Christmas?

A merry Christmas to ewe!

Who's never hungry at Christmas?

The Turkey-he's always stuffed

What did the icy road say to the truck?

Wanna go for a spin?

What is Santa's favourite sport?

The North Pole Vault

What happens when a snowman looses his temper?

He has a meltdown!

Which of Santa's reindeer has the best moves?

Dancer.

What did Adam say the day before Christmas?

It's Christmas, Eve.

What do you call a bankrupt Santa?

Saint Nick-el-less.

What would you call an elf who just has won the lottery?

Welfy

What do you get if you cross a snowman and a baker?

Frosty the Doughman!

What type of motorcycle does Santa ride?

A Holly Davidson.

What do snowmen eat for breakfast?

Frosted Flakes.

Why did the little boy bring his Christmas tree to the hair salon?

It needed a little trim.

What falls at the North Pole and never gets hurt?

Snow.

What kind of photos do elves take?

Elf-ies.

What is it called when Santa takes a break?

A Santa pause.

What do you call an old snowman?

Old Man River!

Why did the Christmas tree go to the barber?

It needed a trim!

How do snowmen get around?

By riding an "icicle!"

What is the best Christmas present?

A broken drum, you just can't beat it.

Merry Christmas
Where is Donald ?

What did the gingerbread man use to fix his house?

Icing.

How did the ornament get addicted to Christmas?

He was hooked on trees his whole life.

What did one ornament say to another?

"I like hanging with you!"

Why did the ornament go to school?

Because it wanted to be "a little brighter"!

Pro Parenting Tip:

Wrap empty boxes and put them under the tree.

Every time your kid acts up throw one in the fire place.

What kind of music do elves like best?

Wrap music.

Why is a foot a good Christmas present?

Because it makes a good stocking filler.

Why is it so cold at Christmas?

Because it's in Decembrrrrrr.

Why did the gingerbread man go to the doctor?

He was feeling crumby.

What do you get if Santa goes down the chimney when a fire is lit?

Krisp Kringle!

How does Darth Vader like his Christmas turkey?

On the dark side!

What do you call a reindeer that tells jokes?

A "comedian"!

Why don't Santa's employees go to the hospital?

They don't have elf care.

What goes Ho, Ho, Ho, thump?

Santa laughing his head off.

What's the difference between the Christmas alphabet and the regular alphabet?

The Christmas alphabet has Noel.

What do snowmen wear on their heads?

Ans. Ice caps!

Why was the snowman looking through the carrots?

He was picking his nose!

Why was the turkey at the North Pole?

To chill out!

How can a snowman lose weight?

He waits until it gets warmer!

What do you call people who are afraid of Santa Claus?

Claustrophobic

Why does Santa Claus go down the chimney on Christmas Eve?

Because it soots him

What do you call a snowman party?

A snowball!

Why did the elf put his bed next to the fireplace?

He wanted to sleep like a log.

What do you call a chicken at the North Pole?

Lost.

How do snowmen get around?

By riding an "icicle!"

What's a snowman's favorite cereal?

Frosted Flakes!

What do you call a cat on the beach during Christmas time?

Sandy Claws!

Why did Santa go to jail?

He sleighed an elf.

Who delivers presents to baby sharks at Christmas?

Santa Jaws!

What do you call an elf that can sing?

A wrapper.

My Earl Grey
tea is
delightful...

Earl Grey

I believe it's time to go...

Make it so, make it so, make it so!

Why dosen’t Santa buy toys from China?

The North Pole doesn't import presents because it is Elf Sufficient.

Why did people start putting up Christmas trees?

Because people thought it would spruce things up a bit.

What do elves do after school?

Their gnome work.

.

Why did Santa have to attend the Christmas party?

Because his presents were required.

What would you get if you ate the Christmas decorations?

Tinselitis.

What did Mary Poppins want from Santa?

Supercalifragilistic-expialia-snowshoes!

WHY YOU STALLING, SANTA?
YOU GONNA START THE
GAME OR NOT?
TAP TAP
V E N I S O N

Why don’t Reindeer don't go to public school?

Because they’re elf taught.

Where is Santa Claus' favourite swimming pool.

The North Pool.

How do you know Santa is good at karate?

He has a black belt!

What do you get when you cross Santa with a duck?

A Christmas Quacker.

What is Santa's favourite kind of candy?

Jolly Ranchers

What do you call Santa when he loses his pants?

Saint Knickerless!

Why did the boy go fishing on Christmas Eve?

He was angling for presents!

What do you get when you cross a snowman and a vampire?

Frostbite!

What's red and white and falls down chimneys?

Santa Klutz!

What is invisible and smells like milk and cookies?

Santa's burps!

What is green, covered with tinsel and goes "ribbit ribbit"?

A mistle-"toad"!

What kind of ball doesn't bounce?

A snowball!

What do reindeer hang on their Christmas trees?

"Horn"-aments!

What's a snowman's favorite snack?

Ice Krispie treats!

What does the Christmas tree say to the light bulb when it’s sad?

Lighten up!

What kind of key can't open locks?

A turkey!

How does Santa keep track of all the fireplaces he's visited?

He keeps a log!

What do you get if you cross a bell with a skunk?

Jingle smells!

What do you call a messy dog at Christmas?

Sandy Paws!

I was afraid this would happen...

Find the Panda Challenge:

Lazy way to win at Christmas decorating

Knock Knock Jokes For Kids

Knock, knock!

Who's there?

Ya.

Ya who?

Wow, you're really excited about Christmas!

Knock, knock!

Who's there?

Noah.

Noah who?

Noah good Christmas joke?

Knock, knock!
    Who's there?
Doughnut.
    Doughnut who?
Doughnut open until Christmas!

Knock, knock!
    Who's there?
Chris.
    Chris who?
Christmas is here!

Knock, knock!
Who's there?
Pudding.
Pudding who?
Pudding up the Christmas lights!

Knock, knock!
Who's there?
Howard.
Howard who?
Howard you like to sing
Christmas carols with me?

Knock, knock!

Who's there?

Coal. Coal who?

Coal me when you hear Santa.

Knock Knock!

Who's there?

Mary.

Mary who?

Mary Christmas!

Knock, knock!
Who's there?
Hannah.
Hannah who?
Hannah partridge in a pear tree.

Knock, knock!
Who's there?
Olive.
Olive who?
Olive the other reindeer.

Knock, knock!
    Who's there?
Luke.
    Luke who?
Luke at all those presents!

Knock, knock!
    Who's there?
Ho Ho.
    Ho Ho who?
That Santa impression needs work.

Knock, knock!
   Who's there?
Holly.
   Holly who?
Holly-days are the best days.

Knock, knock!
   Who's there?
Gladys.
   Gladys who?
Gladys Christmas, aren't you?

Knock, knock!

Who’s there?

Anna.

Anna who?

Anna partridge in a pear tree.

Knock knock.

Who's there?

Snow.

Snow who?

Snow use - I've forgotten my name!

Name Santa's Reindeer Challenge

Can you list the names of all ten of Santa's Reindeer? I bet you forget the name of the second most famous one.

_________ _________ _________

_________ _________ _________

_________ _________ _________

____

The answer is on the last page of the book.

How to tell you've been
REALLY BAD

Name Santa's Reindeer challenge answer page:

Dasher Dancer Prancer

Vixen Comet Cupid

Donner Blitzen Rudolph

Olive

I bet you forgot Olive, the other reindeer. You know the one that all the other reindeer used to laugh and call him names!

www.ingramcontent.com/pod-product-compliance
Lightning Source LLC
Chambersburg PA
CBHW071611040426
42452CB00008B/1309
* 9 7 8 1 7 3 6 1 2 1 4 2 9 *